# LEADERSHIP IN A BOX

# The First Date

**By**

**Andréa Carter**

*Leadership In A Box-The First Date*
ISBN 978-0-692-66175-8
Copyright @2016 by Lulu Publishing

Creative Concept by Andréa Carter

# Table of Contents

_____

# Introduction

Throughout my career, one of the most challenging aspects of my many roles has been leadership. People often look at being a leader or having responsibility for teams as "business" and for the most part, this is an accurate assessment. However, there is something deeper involved in leadership. Anytime there is a relationship between people, there is a certain chemistry that comes into play. It is a little like dating. Think about it. Often times our working relationships last longer than those in our personal lives do.

Today, there are many available options when attempting to identify a significant other. There are clubs, bars, grocery stores, churches and a plethora of dating sites, which have become extremely popular. One has the opportunity to build a profile that best describes who they are with the sole purpose of attracting potential suitors. These profiles include likes & dislikes, hobbies, interests, religious beliefs, etc. Obviously, in the world of business we do not have a dating profile of sorts.

A working relationship is like an arranged marriage. Someone else (matchmaker, website, well-meaning grandmother) has decided that this person has the qualities that would make for a good partner. You do not know them and they do not know you, and yet now, your fortunes are tightly linked. These people are connected and expected to make it work. Therefore, your job from the outset is to make a good impression that is authentic.

You cannot do what you do when it is just a date… send your "date-self representative". You know the one that does not laugh too loud or eat too much and finds everything said fascinating. You have to show up as your true self. Because you are theirs and they are yours. If you do not click at the end of the date, you move on.  Not as easy when you are the leader of a team and are accountable for not only your success but theirs as well.

In reality, the "courting" truly begins once we have landed the job. I get to know you and you get to know me. Everything else before landing the job is like getting dressed for the date. A business relationship is a little different from others because it is not that easy to walk away should you find that there is no chemistry. There is no unfollowing them on social media outlets, blocking their number, and bad mouthing them to everyone you know.  When you are looking for another job, nine times out of ten they will call the previous employer to find out how you were in that relationship.

You see the impact here is far greater than spending a weekend alone, or not having a date for the next big event or function on your calendar. Walking away from business relationships can have a negative financial impact as well as career implications.

You can use this book as a tool to creatively introduce yourself to your new team or colleagues. Think of Leadership in a Box as your dating profile guide. Using the tips in this book, you will understand the importance of being an open book with your team and letting them get to know who you are as a leader from the beginning. Leadership in a Box encapsulates all of your leadership skills into…you guessed it, a box. This exercise will illuminate your creativity and force you to reflect on who you are as a leader. You may even discover some new things about *you* along the way.

## Retrospect

As I reflected on prior roles and teams that I have led, I focused on the connectivity between others and myself on the team. I recalled those first introductory meetings. Some of them were one on one and others were the "inaugural staff meetings." In each of those meetings, I shared a lot about my background and some information about who I was as a person. You see, once I had the job I was okay letting people know that I was married with two daughters because I was taking the personable route. I thought that my approach was clever:  This is "who I am" and this is "what I do."  I was letting some walls down so that my team could feel a little closer to me. I wanted to fine the balance between a great leader and a good colleague. What I noticed was that this still did not provide enough insight to my leadership style. The introductions I gave kind of felt like a speed date that was straight to the point and without any depth to them.  The team actually did not truly begin to understand who I was as a leader until 6 months into the "relationship."

Based on the business strategy and the goals ahead of this team, I did not have the luxury of time. How could I shorten our courting period? I wanted this group to know, understand and respect who I am a lot sooner and vice versa. So how do we creatively share with our new team, who we are; what inspires us; what makes us tick; and what ticks us off? That is a question that I spent a lot of time contemplating. Should I make a slide show? I could take this approach, but it was not creative. Should I suggest a team retreat? Umm, I really do not want to blow my budget in my first week. I thought about countless ways to make the "first date" with my team

count. The more they know in the beginning,

the least likely for surprises later down the

road.

As I was starting a new role in an

iconic organization, I wanted to take a

different approach to introducing myself to

not just my direct reports but to my peers and

colleagues. It was then, that I came up with

Leadership in a Box. Leadership in a Box is a

creative way for leaders in any organization to

share their Style Profile. I spent several

weeks prior to my start date identifying

objects that I felt described something about my leadership style or me. I packaged these items in very nice boxes, even adding a red ribbon, and presented them to my team.

So the day finally arrives. While I am excited, I must admit I am just a little nervous. I am leading my first "all hands" meeting with the new team. There are about thirty-five people in the room. Everyone is present, including my executive assistant. In front of everyone is a copy of the agenda for the meeting and a nice blue gift box with a red ribbon. I will never forget the level of chatter and excitement in the room. Murmurs of what was in the box and how thoughtful I was to get them a gift tickled me but also made me feel just a little guilty because I knew that once they opened the box they would be a bit confused and maybe even a little disappointed. It was not a "please like your new boss" gift. When they opened the box, confused looks and side eyes filled the room. Well here it goes!

## The Box

The box is such a simple concept. So simple, I was pleasantly surprised that my team really enjoyed this unique way of introducing myself. While it is simplistic, it is symbolic as well. The correlation of the items to style lends to the symbolism. The complexity is in how creative you are in representing each item as your leadership traits. No pun intended, but think outside of the box! View it as though it was your dating profile on one of the many online dating sites. When you set up your profile, you choose your very best pictures, answer the surveys, and in your "About Me" section you carefully dot your I's and cross your T's. You are your own marketing executive.

Spend the bulk of your time on what is inside of the box. I hate to say this because it is such a cliché but "It's not about what's on the outside that matters, but what's on the inside." When presenting the box to the team, be mindful that at first they will think you are giving them some kind of, "I'm your new boss and I hope you like me" offering. Therefore, do not spend too much time focusing on how the outside will look. A simple, plain gift box and a ribbon or bow to top it off or a simple gift bag will suffice. Build the anticipation to opening the box. Talk about how much time you put into the gift and why it is important to give the team this special gift. Once my team opened my simple box they found items that represented the "positive" traits which included a slinky, a mirror, a pair of sunglasses, a small canvas with paint, and a bag of assorted candy in a clear cellophane bag. If you read the list and seem a bit confused… good! I will describe what each one symbolizes.

First, we will begin with the slinky, which has a few definitions. The adjective is graceful and sinuous in movement. The next, which everyone is most familiar with, is a toy consisting of a flexible spring that can do somersaults down stairs. I took from both definitions when comparing my leadership skill to the slinky. It represents flexibility and nimbleness. As a leader, I am able to quickly adjust to different situations or environments. We all know that this loveable toy bends and tangles but it does not break. Like a rambunctious child playing with a slinky, I explained that difficult situations will occur, there will be chaos, disengagement, ambiguity, but how well you handle these situations and how well you come back after all is said and done will demonstrate your degree of flexibility. How well do you bounce back? Find an item that represents tenacity and how flexible you can be as a leader.

Next up in my box was the mirror. When you step in front of the mirror the first thing you see is yourself. This is about reflection and being introspective. There will, without a doubt, be times when things go wrong or balls drop. Hold the mirror up instead of pointing fingers. I shared with my team that I hold myself accountable first. What do you own in this? What could you have done differently? How will you correct it going forward? A leader must constantly ask these questions. Accountability is important for any leader because it demonstrates responsibility. The mirror is a demonstration to your team that if you, the leader are holding yourself accountable then they should do the same. Not only that, but we will need to hold each other accountable. I like to call this collective accountability.

Next, the team finds in the box, a pair of sunglasses. "Finally a gift I can use," they will think to themselves and maybe this is true. They can use the sunglasses on a sunny day, but the use for these sunglasses is more than protection from UV rays. Sunglasses are also used to hide or disguise something. We constantly see celebrities with huge sunglasses to hide their faces from the paparazzi or maybe someone is wearing a pair to cover a black eye. However, the sunglasses in the box represent the complete opposite. As a leader you are not there to hide yourself, you are there show up. We do not run from the spotlight. We are in it every day, whether we want to be or not. So why not put your best foot forward. Integrity is what the shades symbolize. You are honest with whom you are and what you think you can bring to the team. I am unapologetic for who I am as a person and as a leader. Now I am not perfect and for that, I do not apologize but I do make strides to become better. I encouraged my team to be who they are. That is integrity to me.

Integrity allows the person to be whole and therefore team is whole.

Now the team is starting to get the hang of it and from the looks on their faces, they appreciate my creative introduction. After finding out how important flexibility, accountability and integrity are to me as a leader, the puzzle piece was next out of the box. Each puzzle piece is unique and when each is placed accordingly, it creates a collective work of art. The puzzle piece symbolizes how important collaboration is to me. Everybody has something to bring to the table. Puzzle pieces do not represent the perfect cookie cutter image, yet each piece compliments one another. I encouraged my team to bring their uniqueness to this new relationship because it is highly appreciated. Just like when you are putting a puzzle together, sometimes certain pieces just do not fit with the other; however, each piece has a specific space designed just for it. No one piece is more important than the other. Everyone has something to offer and each offering is needed.

With four items down, my team pulls out their next "gift". This gift was like a two for one special, a canvas with a paintbrush. These two items show my team that as a new "couple" we have a clean slate. What happened before me does not matter. No, I am not the date that will ask you about all of your exes and what happened and why. That is not me. I will evaluate them on their performance and what is demonstrated from this moment on. As their new leader, I am giving them a chance to create, or recreate, the perception of themselves. Sometimes, especially in personal relationships, things do not work out because of the ghosts of the past. I promise that what I think about them is in their own hands as they are holding the miniature canvas and paintbrush. With me, they have a fresh start and I encourage them to give each other and even themselves a fresh start and forget the past because only the present moment matters. If they decide to paint me a picture, that is a plus as well.

Now, I am sure that someone on your team has a sweet tooth. Given that, I am sure they will appreciate the next item. A cellophane bag with carefully picked assorted candy represents our relationship as a whole. In the bag are Hershey Kisses, bubble gum, Laffy Taffy, Sweet Tarts, Red Hots and Lemon Heads. Candy such as the chocolate and bubble gum represents the days that are smooth sailing. These are times when things are going well and it feels as if we are on a sugar high. These days will be a breeze and the days my team will like me most. It is all good!

The Sweet-tarts represent the days in between sweet and sour. These are the days where balance is vital because the day could go either way. There may be tons of work to do, critical deadlines looming or budget issues arise.  Now, if we keep our heads and a positive mindset, the day can turn out to be sweet. However if on that same day, everyone is stressing, patience is short, tongues are sharp and negative energy is oozing out  into the atmosphere, then the day can turn sour in a blink of an eye. The Red Hots and Lemon Heads represent the times where as a leader, I may say something that you do not like or give you a task to do that will upset you or you may question.  These are for certain the days when things will be a little rough.   In fact, these are the times when my team will likely question my leadership or I may question their level of engagement. But every relationship has challenging times, right?

Finally yet importantly is the clear cellophane bag. This is actually more significant than the candy. I explained that the bag represents transparent communication. Given that this is a budding relationship, we will build upon this foundation. I promised to be as concise and clear with them and hoped that in return that they would do the same. Now clear and concise is not synonymous with curt and rude. There is a difference.

Honesty and communication in any

relationship is key! For example, things are

always easy during the good times however if

I do something to hurt their feelings I need

them to communicate that with me. If I do not

see a problem, how can I respond differently?

Now that you have some inspiration,

think about what you would place in your

leadership box. When leading everyone has

his or her own style, so make your box your

own. You do not have to use any of the items

described above, however if you do, feel free

to change the meaning. Sit down and reflect

on who you are as a leader and present it to

your team.

got purpose?

## Purpose

Have you heard about the Cupcake Stage in a relationship? Most of the time, this stage happens when you and a person skip the courting step of dating and get right into a relationship. You and your partner are on cloud nine and cannot get enough of one another. Little to no arguments takes place in this stage because you both are smitten. Your rose-colored glasses are glued to your face and this new relationship has you on a love high. After six months to a year has passed, you two have seen more sides of each other and spent enough time to know what irritates you about that person.

The arguments are more frequent and you look forward to alone time.

So what does the Cupcake Stage in a relationship have to do with Leadership in a Box? Well, the purpose of Leadership in a box is that your "partner", aka your team, knows everything they need to know about you from the beginning so the dynamics of your relationship will be consistent and harmonious. It is symbolic of courting, instead of jumping right into the relationship. Down the road there will be little to no surprises that will catch your partner off guard.

As a leader, you are not only sharing your strengths with your new team, but you are also exposing your flaws and what makes you fall short sometimes. Your transparency makes the transition from courting to the relationship smoother. Ample information is exchanged between you and your team so that your relationship has a solid foundation to build upon. It is not built on the high of anticipating the experience of something new.

In the work place, there is a constant need to "be on." That means that you are always putting your best foot forward. We believe that this is what it takes to make it to the next level. Focusing on your weakness can be hard and sharing those opportunities can be more of a challenge. A necessary trait to being a great leader, is accepting that you are not perfect and that there is still room for learning and improvement. It is easy to share with anyone what makes you great. Who does not love talking about what makes them above average? However, if you put only good things in your box, you might appear as disingenuous to your team. That is the last the impression that you want to give. So with the box, add items that shine a light on your flaws as well. With your flaws being shared, you are letting your team know what you are working on to become a better, fit leader for them.

Leadership in a Box, allows you to analyze and love what makes you a great leader before anyone else can. So, while you are assembling the boxes for your team, without realizing it you are becoming more comfortable with whom you are as a leader and you are ready to show people why you are capable of leading them. It allows time for you to reflect on your leadership skills and how to offer them you your new team.

# Conclusion

As I walk around the office today, it brings a smile to my face to see that team members still have some of the items from the box. Whether it was the mini mirror hanging on their computers, the shades and slinky sitting on their desk or the easel pinned to their bulletin board, it proved to me that the box had a lasting impact and it was not just cool in that moment. I see every item around the office except the candy because come on, who does not get a sweet tooth every now and then while they are at work. The box certainly influenced them and they begin to apply the meaning to each item in their work life.  Yes, there are times that we have to remind each other of certain items and the meaning. But for the most part, the symbolism has not only resonated but is highly demonstrative amongst the team.

  The box is like timeless gift you give your significant other, a gift you know they will always use or keep near.

    With Leadership in a Box, remember that once your team unties the ribbon and opens the box, they are peeling back the layers of who their new boss will be; you are an open book and there is no turning back.  While this is not to imply that you are a gift to your new team, your goal is to be a light so that you can lead them to

success. You want your team to know and

respect you enough to trust your leadership

skills. Therefore, you have to be transparent

enough with yourself to be able to share who

you are as a leader to your team. As with any

relationship, there is a beginning, a middle and

end. This marks the beginning. Are you ready

for the next stage?

Will you be
my girlfriend

yes    no

Do you want to go steady?

www.ingramcontent.com/pod-product-compliance
Lightning Source LLC
Chambersburg PA
CBHW032020190326
41520CB00007B/557